Forza
Beginner's Guide

21st Century Skills **INNOVATION LIBRARY**

Josh Gregory

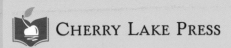
CHERRY LAKE PRESS

Published in the United States of America by Cherry Lake Publishing Group
Ann Arbor, Michigan
www.cherrylakepublishing.com

Reading Adviser: Beth Walker Gambro, MS, Ed., Reading Consultant, Yorkville, IL

Cherry Lake Press is an imprint of Cherry Lake Publishing Group.

Library of Congress Cataloging-in-Publication Data

Names: Gregory, Josh, author.
Title: Forza : beginner's guide / Josh Gregory.
Description: Ann Arbor, Michigan : Cherry Lake Publishing, [2024] | Series:
    Unofficial guides | Includes bibliographical references and index. |
    Audience: Grades 4-6 | Summary: "For twenty years, the Forza franchise
    has been one of the most successful racing game series in the world. In
    this book, readers will learn about Forza's fascinating history and
    discover all the driving tips they need to finish in first place.
    Includes table of contents, author biography, sidebars, glossary, index,
    and informative backmatter"— Provided by publisher.
Identifiers: LCCN 2024035821 (print) | LCCN 2024035822 (ebook) | ISBN
    9781668956458 (hardcover) | ISBN 9781668957301 (paperback) | ISBN
    9781668958179 (epub) | ISBN 9781668959916 (ebook) | ISBN 9781668960622
    (kindle edition) | ISBN 9781668959046 (pdf)
Subjects: LCSH: Forza video games—Juvenile literature. | Racing—Juvenile
    literature. | Video games—Juvenile literature.
Classification: LCC GV1469.35.F72 G74 2024 (print) | LCC GV1469.35.F72
    (ebook) | DDC 794.8—dc23/eng/20240814
LC record available at https://lccn.loc.gov/2024035821
LC ebook record available at https://lccn.loc.gov/2024035822

Cherry Lake Press would like to acknowledge the work of the Partnership for 21st Century Learning, a Network of Battelle for Kids. Please visit Battelle for Kids online for more information.

Printed in the United States of America

Note from publisher: Websites change regularly, and their future contents are outside of our control.
Supervise children when conducting any recommended online searches for extended learning opportunities.

Josh Gregory is the author of more than 200 books for kids. He has written about everything from animals to technology to history. A graduate of the University of Missouri–Columbia, he currently lives in Chicago, Illinois.

Contents

CHAPTER 1

Road Warriors

Few things are as exciting as zooming around a racetrack at top speed. You can feel the power of the race car rumbling around you. Ahead of you are the opponents you need to pass. Coming up behind are opponents who want to pass *you*. Every little thing you do makes a difference in the race. When will you hit the brakes or speed up? When will you try to pass the car in front of you? At what angle will you turn into the next curve?

Car racing is a thrilling experience. But most people never get to do it in real life. Race cars are rare and expensive. It takes a lot of training to learn how to drive one safely. And if you're young, you probably don't even know how to drive a regular car yet!

Video games allow players to experience all kinds of things they can't do in real life. So it's no surprise that car racing games have been one of the most popular game **genres** since the very beginning. Some of the earliest video games were based on racing. They go all the way back to the 1970s! These early games were very simple. They weren't anything like driving a real car. But computers started getting a lot more powerful.

If you've ever wondered what it's like to drive a Porsche, the Forza games are a safe way to find out.

3
54
MPH

In Forza games, the interiors of cars are just as detailed as the exteriors.

In the late 1980s, some **developers** started creating more realistic racing games. These **simulation** games, or sims, were meant to re-create the experience of driving a real car. Real-life driving is all about being careful, even at high speeds. These games included all the features of real cars. They required people to really learn how their virtual cars worked. Winning required strategy and patience. But other racing games didn't try to be realistic at all. These arcade-style racers aimed to create the feeling of going as fast as possible at all times.

By the 1990s there were all kinds of racing games in both categories. But playing racing sims at home generally required a powerful PC and special racing controllers. Players on home consoles mostly enjoyed arcade-style games like *Mario Kart* or *Ridge Racer*. That all changed in 1997. That year, Sony released *Gran Turismo* for the PlayStation console. *Gran Turismo* had all the realism and detail of a sim. But it was also fun for the average person to play. It didn't require a fancy PC. This helped make it a massive hit.

In 2001, Microsoft released the first Xbox game console. The *Gran Turismo* series was only available for Sony's PlayStation systems. Microsoft wanted its own realistic racing game that could compete with *Gran Turismo*. It started up a new game development team called Turn 10 Studios. In 2005, they released their first game, *Forza Motorsport*. It had all the realism of games like *Gran Turismo*. But it also had the flashy fun of arcade-style racing games. It was a massive hit, and it kicked off a whole series of Forza games.

The Forza games are known for their cutting-edge graphics.

The Forza series is still going strong more than 20 years later. It has sold millions and millions of copies. You have probably played at least one of these games yourself if you like racing. But where do you start if you are new to the series? And how do you go from a beginner to an expert racer? It will take some practice. But soon you'll be cruising around the track like a pro driver.

Forza on the Go

So far, the only way to play the main Forza games has been on a TV or computer monitor. But Microsoft has also released a couple of spinoff games for mobile devices. *Forza Street* was a game based around street racing. It was much simpler than the main Forza games. It also didn't last long. The game was only available from 2020 until 2022.

In 2023, Microsoft also released *Forza Customs*. This mobile game doesn't have any racing at all. Instead, it's all about solving puzzles. Doing this lets players customize their race cars.

These games might not have the detailed racing action of the main Forza series. But they can offer a taste of the excitement for players on the go.

CHAPTER 2

In the Driver's Seat

Driving a car might seem simple enough if you've never tried it. You push on one pedal (or a button in a video game) to go faster. You push another to hit the brakes and slow down. You turn a wheel to steer. But driving a car correctly is a lot more complex than it might seem at first. And it's even more complex when you are driving a powerful car at high speed!

Every car is different. Cars have different shapes. They weigh different amounts. Some are heavier in the front than they are in the back. They have different kinds of engines. Some cars are rear-wheel drive. This means the engine powers the back wheels. The car gets pushed forward. Other cars are front-wheel drive. The engine powers the front wheels. They pull the car forward. Some cars **accelerate** more quickly than others. Others might have higher top speeds. These are just some of the things that can affect the way a car handles.

One of the things that makes Forza games stand out is that they are packed with hundreds of real-life cars. Each in-game car is designed to handle exactly like the real-life version. This means you get to enjoy the experience of driving all kinds of interesting cars.

Each Forza game is packed with incredibly detailed models of real-life cars.

SILVERSTONE RACING CIRCUIT

Silverstone

58.4 °F   International Circuit
06:00 PM   Silverstone, England

Ⓐ Skip

Pay attention to the preview videos for each track to get an idea of what kinds of challenges the race will offer.

But it also means you need to learn about different kinds of cars to get good at the game.

The big challenge of racing is to find the best path around each track. Then you have to learn how to make your car follow that path while keeping as high a speed as you can without losing control. You might wonder how there could be different paths along a single racetrack. But even a simple oval-shaped track can have many different paths. It all comes down to the way you make each turn or curve.

Generally the best way to make a turn is to start out on the outer edge of the track. You want to slow the car down before you start the turn. The tighter the turn, the slower you need to be. You won't be able to make a sharp turn while going fast. But don't slam on the brakes all at once. This could make you lose control.

After slowing down, turn toward the inner edge of the curve. You will slowly let off the brakes. You might coast for a little bit. As your car reaches the center

Behind the Wheel

The simplest way to enjoy Forza and other racing games is to play using a controller. But many Forza fans want the experience to be as real as possible. They get special racing controllers to play the game. These can include steering wheels, pedals, and a stick for shifting gears. Some serious players even build cockpits they can sit inside as they play.

point of a turn, you will accelerate again. The idea is to slow down as the turn begins, then increase speed as the turn ends. This might sound easy. But getting a feel for it can be tricky at first. Each car will react differently. Each turn is different. And some turns will go right into other turns. It will take a lot of practice to get used to all of this. If you don't get it right, you will drive off the track. This will slow you down a lot.

You can see what gear your car is in above your speed in the bottom-right corner.

Other cars will also be on the track as you're trying to turn. You should try not to bump into them. No one will get hurt, because it's a video game. But it will slow you down. It could even cause you to lose control of your car and spin off the road. Learning when to try to pass other cars and when to stay behind them is an important part of racing. Once again, it will take practice to get a good feel for this.

Most race cars have a manual **transmission**. Engines have different gears in them. Have you ever ridden a bike with gears? At a low gear, it is easy to pedal. But you don't go very fast. At a high gear, you can go much faster. But pushing the pedals is hard if you don't already have some speed. Car engines work a lot like this. Drivers shift into higher gears at different speeds. This gives them more control over the car. But it also makes driving more complicated. You need to shift down before each turn. Then you shift back up when you start to accelerate.

The developers of Forza know it can be a challenge to learn the basics of racing. So their games have guide features to help players get better. One of them is a line that appears on the track in front of your car.

Pay attention to the on-track guide as you are learning a new course. When it's red, you need to slow down!

The guide line shows you a good path to take along the course. It also changes color to show when you should brake or accelerate. The feature is turned on when you first start the game. It is best to leave it on until you have improved your skills. Then you can turn it off and try coming up with your own strategies.

Top Forza players learn how to drive with a manual transmission. But if you are just starting out, you can leave your car's transmission on automatic. The game will shift gears for you as you drive. This will make it harder for you to win against the very best players online. But you should do fine if you are playing in single-player mode.

Practice is the key to getting better at driving in real life. The same is true in Forza. Keep trying a track until you learn every detail. Drive different types of cars and get a feel for them. Soon you won't even have to think as you zip from one turn to the next. It will all feel natural.

CHAPTER 3

Motorsport Madness

Are you looking for realistic racing action? *Forza Motorsport* is the series for you. This is the main Forza series. It focuses on sim-style racing. Many of the tracks in these games are based on real-life race locations. Each one contains detailed models of hundreds of real-life cars. You will learn a lot about real-life car racing just from playing the game.

So far, there have been eight *Forza Motorsport* games. The first seven games are all numbered sequels. But the latest one is simply called *Forza Motorsport*. It's the same title as the original game from 2005. But this new game was released in 2023. And it is the biggest, most detailed Forza game yet.

Cars are made up of many, many different parts. A big part of racing is making **upgrades** and adjustments to these parts. Some changes improve a car's overall performance. For example, you might tweak a car's engine to give it more overall power. Its top speed will improve. Other adjustments are done to make the car better in specific situations. For example, different kinds of tires might be better on different tracks or in different weather.

You will feel the difference on the track when driving in the rain.

Similarly, a lot of the fun in Forza comes from collecting and upgrading all kinds of different cars. In *Forza Motorsport,* you will start out by choosing your first car. There are three options. They are the Ford Mustang GT, the Honda Civic Type R, and the Subaru STI S209. You will use this car in your first few races. But soon you will have a garage full of high-end cars to choose from. Some of them can be earned from winning certain races. But others have to be purchased.

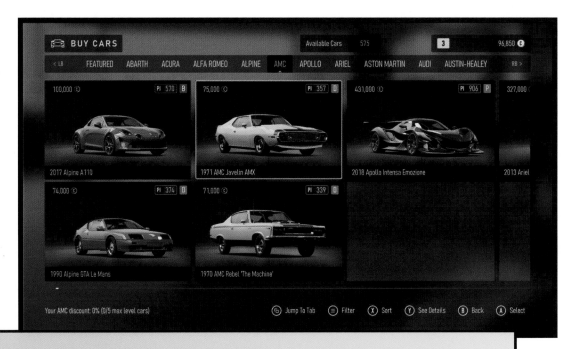

Forza Motorsport offers everything from classic muscle cars to state-of-the-art supercars.

BUY CARS   3   96,850 C

PURCHASE

VIEW CAR

AMC

1971 AMC
Javelin AMX

RWD   PI 357   0

Speed   Braking
1.0   1.2

1.3   2.4
Handling   Acceleration

PRICE   75,000 C

Y Toggle Card   B Back   A Select

You can examine a car and decide whether you really want it before handing over your credits.

As you complete race events, you will earn credits. Credits are your source of money in the game. You can use them to purchase new cars. You can also buy upgrades for the cars you already own. You will need to buy new cars to make progress in the game. You can't just keep using the same one the entire time. Most of the game's race events have rules about which kinds of cars can participate. This keeps things fair. You might be able to bring a car that is a little better than all of the other opponents' cars. But it won't be so much

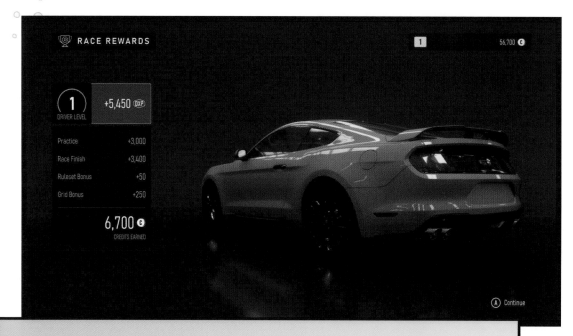

1   56,700 ⓒ

1
DRIVER LEVEL   +5,450 ⓓⓍⓟ

Practice	+3,000
Race Finish	+3,400
Ruleset Bonus	+50
Grid Bonus	+250

6,700 ⓒ
CREDITS EARNED

Ⓐ Continue

You'll earn different amounts of XP and credits depending on how well you raced.

better that you will automatically win. These rules will also keep you from showing up to a race with a car that is impossible to win with.

Completing races will also earn you experience points, or XP. There are two kinds: Car XP and Driver XP. Car XP will build up to gain levels for the specific car you are driving. Leveling up your car allows you to use different kinds of upgrades on that car. You will get more Car XP the better you drive. For example, you will get more XP if you don't bump into any cars or drive off the track.

Driver XP lets you increase your driver level. This level shows your overall progress in the game. Increasing your level will earn you additional cars and credits.

You'll see your Car XP increase in the top-right corner of the screen as you race.

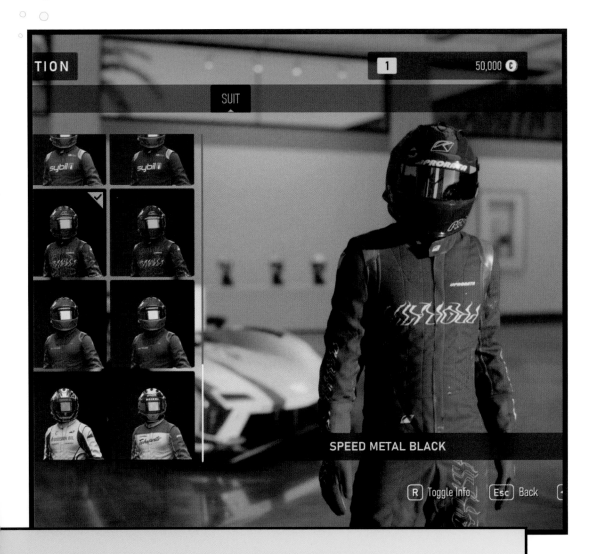

You can even customize the look of your driver.

Where You'll Find Forza

The Forza series was created by Microsoft. For many years it was only playable on Xbox systems. More recent games are also available to play on Windows PCs. If you only have a PlayStation or a Nintendo Switch system, you're out of luck for now. But you never know what the future might hold. Microsoft has started making some of its other game series available for more systems. One day Forza could be playable on other systems.

Upgrades aren't the only way to customize your car in *Forza Motorsport*. You can also change the look of your car with all kinds of patterns and paint colors. You can even change the look of your driver's uniform and helmet. It's a fun way to express your creativity as you play the game. And if you play online, other players will get to see your unique look.

CHAPTER 4

On the Horizon

Do you like your racing a little faster and wilder? Do you want to take your cars off the track and into jungles and up mountainsides? *Forza Horizon* might be more your speed than *Forza Motorsport*. The original *Forza Horizon* game was released in 2012. It was a spinoff of the main *Forza Motorsport* series. It was a big hit. This led Microsoft to start switching back and forth between Motorsport and Horizon games. The latest one is *Forza Horizon 5*, released in 2021.

The Horizon games are developed by a company called Playground Games. They have a lot in common with the main Motorsport series. They feature tons of real-life cars and fast-paced racing action. But they focus on street racing and off-road driving. They are a little more arcade-focused than the Motorsport games.

Cars are easier to steer. You can take corners at higher speeds without losing control. And best of all, you can drive wherever you want.

In *Forza Motorsport*, you choose different race events from a menu. You are taken to the track, and the race begins. Afterward, you go back to the menu. But *Forza Horizon* is different. Horizon games take place in an open world. There is a huge map for you to explore. You will find race events scattered around the world.

GET TO THE BAJA CIRCUIT

173

You can drive anywhere you want to in *Forza Horizon*.

But there are also other kinds of activities. For example, you might be asked to get your car up to a high speed on a certain length of track. Or you might be asked to perform car stunts to earn points. There are even ramps and cliffs that let you send your car flying through the air. All of this is a lot less realistic than anything in *Forza Motorsport*. But it sure is a lot of fun.

You can open up the map and look for new activities to complete any time you're in the open world.

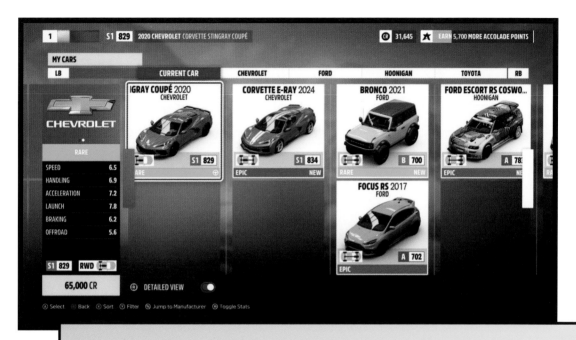

| 1 | | S1 829 | 2020 CHEVROLET CORVETTE STINGRAY COUPÉ | | | | CR 31,645 | ★ | EARN 5,700 MORE ACCOLADE POINTS |

MY CARS

| LB | | CURRENT CAR | CHEVROLET | FORD | HOONIGAN | TOYOTA | RB |

CHEVROLET

RARE

SPEED	6.5
HANDLING	6.9
ACCELERATION	7.2
LAUNCH	7.8
BRAKING	6.2
OFFROAD	5.6

GRAY COUPÉ 2020 CHEVROLET — S1 829 — RARE

CORVETTE E-RAY 2024 CHEVROLET — S1 834 — EPIC NEW

BRONCO 2021 FORD — B 700 — RARE NEW

FORD ESCORT RS COSWO... HOONIGAN — A 78 — EPIC NE

FOCUS RS 2017 FORD — A 702 — EPIC

S1 829 RWD

65,000 CR

R DETAILED VIEW

A Select   B Back   X Sort   Y Filter   N Jump to Manufacturer   R Toggle Stats

Just like *Forza Motorsport*, *Forza Horizon* is packed with real-life cars to unlock.

Forza Horizon even has a storyline. At the start of the game, you get to create and name your own character. Other characters will talk to you as you race. You will meet up with them at different events. You'll watch scenes showing the story develop as you complete more and more events.

Racing against an airplane might not be realistic, but it sure is a lot of fun!

The Forza games are made by people who love cars for other people who love cars. Have you ever dreamed of getting behind the wheel? These games could be the next best thing. And when it comes time to drive for real, you might be surprised at how much you already know!

Dollars and Sense

Some games in the Forza series have in-game shops. This is where you can spend real-world money to unlock new cars and other features. Each of these microtransactions is usually not very expensive on its own. But making a lot of them can really add up. Soon, you could be surprised how much money you've spent on a game. Always ask an adult before spending money in an in-game store. And always be careful that you don't spend more than you can afford!

GLOSSARY

accelerate (ak-SEL-uh-rayt) to increase in speed

developers (dih-VEL-uh-purz) the people who design and program video games or other computer programs

gears (GEERZ) parts of an engine that turn in order to power other parts

genres (ZHAHN-ruhz) categories of games, books, or other forms of media, based around shared features

microtransactions (MYE-kroh-trans-ak-shuhns) things that can be purchased for a small amount of money within a video game or other computer program

simulation (sim-yuh-LAY-shun) a computer program meant to imitate real life

transmission (trans-MISH-uhn) the part of a car's engine that shifts gears

upgrades (UP-grayds) improvements

FIND OUT MORE

Books

Gregory, Josh. *PC Gaming: Beginner's Guide*. Ann Arbor, MI: Cherry Lake Publishing, 2022.

Loh-Hagan, Virginia. *Nerding Out About Gaming*. Ann Arbor, MI: 45th Parallel Press, 2024.

Loh-Hagan, Virginia. *Video Games*. Ann Arbor, MI: 45th Parallel Press, 2021.

Websites

With an adult, learn more online with these suggested searches.

Forza Site
Check out the official Forza website for the latest updates on both the Motorsport and Horizon series.

Forza Wiki
This fan-created site is packed with detailed information about all the games in the Forza series.

INDEX